HARRIET RUBIN'S MOTHER'S WOODEN HAND

Phoenix Poets

A SERIES EDITED BY ROBERT VON HALLBERG

HARRIET RUBIN'S MOTHER'S

WOODEN HAND

SUSAN HAHN

*For Richard —
With many thanks
and best wishes
Susan*

THE UNIVERSITY OF CHICAGO PRESS

Chicago and London

Susan Hahn is associate editor of TriQuarterly *magazine and co-director of* TriQuarterly Books. *Her poems have appeared in journals such as* North American Review, Poetry, Shenandoah, Southern Review, *and* Prairie Schooner. *This is Hahn's first book of poetry.*

The University of Chicago Press, Chicago 60637
The University of Chicago Press, Ltd., London
© 1991 by The University of Chicago
All rights reserved. Published 1991
Printed in the United States of America

00 99 98 97 96 95 94 93 92 91 5 4 3 2 1

Library of Congress Cataloging-in-Publication Data

Hahn, Susan.
    Harriet Rubin's mother's wooden hand / Susan Hahn.
        p.   cm. — (Phoenix poets)
    ISBN 0-226-31299-2 (cloth) — ISBN 0-226-31301-8 (pbk.)
    I. Title.   II. Series.
    PS3558.A3238H37   1991
    811'.54—dc20   90-46443
                                                                        CIP

⊚ *The paper used in this publication meets the minimum requirements of the American National Standard for Information Sciences—Permanence of Paper for Printed Library Materials, ANSI Z39.48–1984.*

For Frederic L.
For Frederic F.

For Jessie and Sol

. . . a time would come when the book would
be written, when it would be behind me,
and I think that a little of its clarity
might fall over my past. Then, perhaps,
because of it, I could remember my life
without repugnance.

—Antoine Roquentin
from *Nausea,* by Jean-Paul Sartre

Acknowledgments

Grateful acknowledgment is made to the editors of publications in which these poems, or versions of them, first appeared:

The North American Review   "Shavings"
Poetry   "Agoraphobia," "Looking Out on Africa," "Melancholia,"
   "Small Green," "Waiting at the Gate," "Flowers"
Poetry East   "At the Intersection," "The Blue Porcelain Bird"
Poetry Northwest   "The Picture I Never Gave Her"
Prairie Schooner   "The Death of a Small Animal"; Reprinted from
   Prairie Schooner by permission of University of Nebraska Press. ©
   1985 University of Nebraska Press
River Styx   "After Chemotherapy," "Feuerstein," "Since Then"
Shenandoah   "Of Tulips and Trillium," "Trichotillomania,"
   "Circumcision"
Southern Poetry Review   "The Tonsure"
The Southern Review   "Amphibians"
TriQuarterly (a publication of Northwestern University) "Given
   Name," "The *Lamedvovniks*," "Psalm"

"Agoraphobia" also appeared in *Sutured Words: Contemporary
   Poetry About Medicine*, Jon Mukand, ed., Aviva Press, 1987.
"Looking Out on Africa," "Waiting at the Gate," "The Death of a

Small Animal," and "The Blue Porcelain Bird" were reprinted in *The Anthology of Magazine Verse & Yearbook of American Poetry*, Alan Pater, ed., Monitor Book Co., 1984, 1985, 1988, 1991.

Contents

Claustrophobia

The feeling started in the womb,
there wasn't room enough
for her.
Voices from the other side
spoke of how they hoped
it was a boy.
She wanted to run,
unravel from the fetal knot,

but couldn't
ease into the narrow
passageway, persuade herself
it was an opening.
So they cut her out
a wider door
and she began careful
not to get too close.
Now, when she's forced

into a crowded place
she always imagines
being stuck in
other people's displeasures.
She returns to a crawlway
full of old alarm
and is caught
angry and unborn.

For Adam, Who, Had He Been Born, Would Have Killed Himself

The sperm that housed half your life slipped up
the tube too soon for the moon-held egg
and instead of you I fell
into this world. Our parents wanted

you and I felt you everywhere,
always rushing at me, your bare feet tramping
on my laces, your fast hands grabbing
my sashes, insistently shoving
me aside. I'd stretch to catch
your ear, so you would have to hear me say
"Adam, I'm tired of your invasions; leave
me alone." Sometimes I'd pretend
you didn't exist. I couldn't imagine

how you'd survive. They believed
you'd give them perfection, make the world
a paradise. I decided it would be best if you were
left where you began—the unripened egg tucked in,
a sperm quickly dissolving undisturbed.

The Blue Porcelain Bird

Lillianne weighed no more than ninety pounds
but every other Friday she'd come to scrub
our floors on all fours and hang half herself
outside our third-story windows to wash
the glass, her delicate hands and arms
flittering in the sun
as she balanced on the sill.
Sometimes I'd mime her with a pretend dustcloth,
try to be as agile and she'd giggle
as if she had a private joke. She only spoke
to answer, and then her voice was even
like a hum. When she'd finish
my grandmother would make sure everything
was intact, from the tiny figurines in the living room
to the loose change in her own latched purse.

After Lillianne would leave, the cup and dish
she used for lunch were scoured, then buried
back in the deepest corner
of a kitchen shelf, and each time
they were hidden a temptation rose in me
until I insisted I'd only eat from them.
Instead, my mother let me
hold the blue porcelain bird—
the one always looked for
first when Lillianne was done.
As I cradled the graceful shape
and traced the line of its smooth throat,
she forked the food into my mouth and snapped
how lucky I was for the meat
on my table and that I wasn't born crippled
or *shvartz*. I couldn't grasp the first parts
of what she said the way I could the last
and, frightened that it would slip off my lap,
I gripped the bird with both hands and held fast.

Trichotillomania

Mother twisted every action
to suit her mother's mood,
which ran from sour to bittersweet.
Mother only had one motion of her own—
she picked
her scalp as if searching for the right
hair would lessen
all the tension. I'd watch

her hand curlicue into a question
mark, tear out the nervous
answer, examine what
she plucked, toss her head,
then pat it
as she would to soothe
my sister's in the crib.
Once I brought a tweezer
to help her

grab what I thought
she wanted. She let me explore
the ruins underneath her beauty
shop creation. I touched
the sores and stubble, tried to
yank out all the trouble
until she yelled

to stop. From then I never could.
I keep looking for the spot
on my own head, ask anyone
who will to rub.
When I'm alone,
I use two mirrors, struggle
to see if I can get hold
of the anxiety. Deep within
my skull a stem is snarling
and will split the bone.

Harriet Rubin's Mother's Wooden Hand

She wore a black glove over it
to cover such terrible
bad luck.
But I knew all
the witch stories and was prepared
not to eat anything
she offered or touched.
I'd run home always Snow White
before the poisoned apple.

My grandmother would say how odd,
that hand missing and her
not having a husband either.
I'd wonder which happened first,
if one had caused the other—what magic
might make both reappear.
I'd fit it all into a fairy tale
until finally I stopped
playing in their apartment.
Everything there grieved
and told me no matter
what I wished
someday I too would vanish.

Melancholia

Death's ill-tempered daughter
is unlike others
who hopscotch off
returning only
when they've run out
of games.
She stays close

squirming
in a stony lap
whining
from discomfort
yet never leaving home.
Her room is crowded
with philosophies
psychologies
and pills

and a mother forever
wandering in and out
checking
her favorite
child.

The Tonsure

At nine years, she styled one on herself
that no one could see, stroking it
at night as it eased her
into sleep against the rumple
and the odor of her aunt's sheets.
It made the wait become a dream
so when her father carried her to the cot
in the dining room, after the grown-ups
were finished with their dinnertime fights,
she'd wake for just a moment
then slip into the fresh
quiet of the room. Her place

had no door, just a stucco portico
that exposed the living room,
where everything was sealed
in plastic so it would keep forever
clean. Mornings the bed was folded
and pushed into a crowded closet
among the overcoats, where she'd hide
sometimes and whisper to the silent
figures, loosen her hair, show them the secret—

the small full moon shape.
It seemed another way out
of her body, unlike her mouth or lower parts,
allowing her to attach herself
to a soothing from above.
In her mind she'd dance and sing
as her fingers shined
its surface until it began to bleed

and her mother pleaded with silver
dollars, one for each week she'd keep
her hands off of it. And she agreed,
for it ached too much to touch.
Still, at night in the soiled bed
she'd picture its symmetry, its silky face,
and caressing a coin collected for being good,
she'd pretend she held, and was, a perfect world
turning slowly in a tranquil space.

The Lamedvovniks

*According to Jewish folklore, there are thirty-six
righteous men who live unrecognized in every
generation and by whose merit the world is able to
continue its existence.*

—*The New Jewish Encyclopedia*

My mother's convinced her father
with his calm manner was one,
while my aunt insists
her dead sister with her generous
smile was another. I wonder
how much the Hasidic scholars
would be bothered
that a woman was so considered,
and what they'd say about the boy
who died last night in a subway tunnel
running to retrieve an old woman's purse.
I'm certain she'd include him
in the ennobled number.

Today a friend confides she struck
a parked car, then sped away.
Sick with surprise, she recoils
as if she's spoiled the chance

to be the person that she thought she was
and she asks would I have left
my name and address.
In the background a zealot
speaks softly on TV, guns packed
onto his back, mouth full
of his beliefs. Later a policeman
holds a petty thief, who bows
his head, atones with a melodious
"Bless You" to his captor
and once more, into the microphone.

We watch, adding to and subtracting
from our separate lists,
trying to figure out
who it is who is
allowing the world to exist.

Waiting at the Gate

Ten of us at 6:00 P.M. Fridays
during July and August would wait
against the white wood fence for
our fathers to arrive one by one.
We'd cheer each
out of his driving-tired expression—
at least while he came through
the gate, drove onto the gravel
road, parked and entered the world
of weekday women and children left
to flourish in the country.

All week we spent
with mothers, grandmothers, and aunts,
listened to the possible
dangers of eating summer
berries, the first symptoms
of polio, what the sign
"Fuck the Jews" meant
that someone had scrawled over
"South Haven, Mich., pop. 6000."

Our fathers brought us less
disturbing facts: reasons for being
a Cub or White Sox fan,
why it was important
to own AT&T.
They swelled
the air with smoke
and we wore paper cigar rings
all weekend.

On Sundays they left
without pomp. Each would quietly walk
from his family's cottage,
luggage in hand,
cakes and cookies packed inside.

We'd line up
against the white wood fence and watch
them pull away
onto the concrete road.
They'd leave us
to question how easily they could
be elsewhere
for another five days.

The Woman Who Wrote the Alphabet

Every fourth week on Sunday her father disappears
for the entire day.
When he comes home he shuts
the door to the apartment bathroom,
orders her to leave him alone.
Monday she'll know
to look in the green Packard
for clear candy wrappers and reams
of paper with the alphabet so correctly
penciled over and over.
Someone is sending a message
she can't figure out. He says
at five, she's too young.
When she's ten

she goes with him, visits a woman
who will not look at her no matter
how she smiles, how carefully
she behaves. They eat ice cream
and penny candy in a corner drugstore
but nothing satisfies

the woman who keeps begging
to be taken home. Instead they go back
to a walled-in building and he returns
to the car with only the familiar
rolls of paper
that no one will look at anymore.
She's too scared
to question him.
Years later, when she asks

him something difficult once again
he will not answer and she calls him a bastard.
He makes her apologize to his absent mother
whom she doesn't have in mind at all
when she yells the word. She believes it
the most disturbing punishment designed
to fill her with guilt
that her insult can be felt
by a woman so far away.
But when she recites the sentence
"I apologize to your mother," she sees herself
as the woman who wrote the alphabet, repeating
a message no one would receive.

Schizophrenia

Taken in by designs of witches
on fragile princesses,
as well as by deductive and inductive
methods, I always imagine
everything not exactly

how it's agreed to be.
In an earlier age
they would have burnt me crisp
and some days it seems okay
to be reduced
to ash.
Now, therapists intrigue themselves
when I enlarge
on the meanings
of my life, the matériel
I haul to every intimate war:
the personalities
in what I wear—
the warp the fabric takes—
the dangers for certain

numbers and dates
that go beyond the relatively
harmless 13,
voices that submit to voices.
I try

to meet the world
serenely, prepare as someone
might for an invited guest.
But when I open up
the door, the whole universe
comes whirling past,
dressed in its own
crazy quilt fashioned
in every distressful
hue and I don't know
what to make of it
except what I already do.

Who We Are to Each Other

Dressed only in blue and white
she looked like the sky on a sunny day.
It's only when I came closer,
saw the biblical sayings scrawled
on strips of paper pinned from her collar
down to her hem, heard her
hymn, that I turned
and ran. They said you

too weren't well and now that I've asked
for the hospital records—twenty years
diminished to ten pages—seen
the smug flourish of the psychologist's
script, the mug shot taken—the asylum's
photograph, your hair chopped off,
the blank convict look—
I want so much to call you back to
grandmother. You who once
worked in a bakery, swirled
all those Happy Birthdays out.
At least someone had the grace
to leave that good detail in
among the cremated facts:

the contusions on your limbs
(sometimes I too dig deep into my skin),
how you thought wildflowers grew and hooted,
pricked you through your mattress
(sometimes I too jump
to the blazing perfumed voices).
Though I can rest in a soft bed,
sleep even with the night
terrors—damaged souls that hiss
from the thin walls—the messages

remain half-hidden. Now I search
for the old woman,
need not to be frightened by her
quotes, her moan, so I can travel
to your grave, place more
than a pebble on the stone,
yell above all the noise
that roams your head, try to
understand who we are to each other,
wake up the living, wake up the dead.

The Bookkeeper and His Daughter

Last night I dreamed us dead, watched
the mourners view
you in your glossy business suit,
loud tie and me,
hooded in gray flannel,
my coverlet a red taffeta dress
which my soul slipped into
so your soul could see

me as the cheerful frivolous girl
you always wanted to show off
while you talked of credits,
debits, assets, liabilities.
You didn't teach me how to count

on anything since I didn't turn out
to be a son, but I couldn't
die—though sometimes I'd almost
try with scissors and sashes.
Our brusque kisses goodbye
canceled tentative hellos,
left us minus

each other in my nightmare.
All the Freudian analysts proved wrong,
their issue, desire for sex,
never between us. What we felt
was just a deficit.

Looking Out on Africa

I slept inside a crib
in the corner of my parents' room
until I was six.
I lay between the safety
bars like a baby elephant
looking out on Africa, my parents
always hunting
each other underneath
their sheets.
They'd move into the unknown
territory and there
in that large space of bed
with no visible bars,
I'd hear the secret
noises of discovery
and see the shapes
of pleasure
and of discontent.

I don't remember thoughts
I had.
Memory merges with my own
geometry, becomes part of how
I dance
the foreign dance,
sing
the strange sounds.
All barriers invisible.

Hysteria

I know I know
I took in too much
but the tree was there
with its enticing skins,
the garden intolerably quiet,
the snake so colorful, resolute,
I thought if I could just fondle
the fruit . . . but now, Please God,
I want to go back to the beginning
of the day so I can say no thank you:
it's all considerably more than I can handle.

Memories of the Pleasure

On a train bound west, a silver ring
encircling her finger and a husband
of six hours pressing his palms
against hers, she rose over
him with a desire that held

as long as the weeks
she stayed well. For when a fever
that wasn't passion flared within her, he broke
the sickness vow, left her
for hours—returning only at night
with cardboard containers filled with melting
ice cream which she'd eat to cool herself,
and then, as if they were still on the train,
he'd climb into her. Untroubled

that it wasn't easy, for her body
was limp and wet, sometimes he'd slip
away while she lay waiting
for the day she'd leave him for good—
her rage stronger than his courting
words that no one would love her more
and the sweet times she'd agree

to be touched in a place she'd never been.
When she escaped, she rode
the eastward train alone,
frayed, as memories of the pleasure
tangled and untangled themselves
with memories of the pain.

Circumcision

When she dreams, she's agile
handles his skin with ease
considers whether she should
fold the flap before
she brings her lips closer.
She's only known Jewish
men. O Freud

would have liked to play
in her mind,
maybe even laughed
after she left, certainly
taken copious notes: *doctor*
I've never felt my father's
love, but when I was six
we took a bath together.
Curious, I moved
toward him and he jumped,
slapped my fingers; the water
stung my wide open
eyes. A member

of the Analytic Society lives
up the block from her.
Once they met; his face blazed
as he offered her his knowledge—
his empty couch, hot
in the attic of his tri-level
house. When she walks by
he reappears, hovers
near his tree, hoping

she'll come inside.
She used to go five times a week
to a man who waited in his
garage, converted into an office.
The exhaust remained long past
the day he asked her to accept
his own sins and she gulped and rushed
home afterward to vomit.
Now she just audits courses,

rests the tender nerves
in her lower
back, injured when she reached
clumsily in bed. This stifling
summer she sits in on
"Ancient Greek Psychology."
The syllabus suggests
Aristotle's *De Amina Bks. II & III*
Nietzsche's *The Birth of Tragedy*
Foucault's *The Use of Pleasure.*
The other students in the class,
a dancer who paints herself to appear
like a mime and a quiet
suburban girl with a deepening

tan, are young enough
to be her daughters,
though there's still a man who'd fly
3000 miles if she'd just imply
she'd open her limbs to him.
But she's done
away with superfluous

motion. Instead she ruminates on if
she should truss
the cover with her thumb
before she attaches
to the lover in her fantasies—
a man for whom she'd risk her spine—
lies down with pain and contemplates
what's real, what's sublime.

What She Saw, What She Thought

Her eyes catch the cinder
block walls inside
the woman's apartment, the solitary
chair, its stuffing
half torn out, the woman's bruises.
Frightened, she turns
the TV off, chooses
pearls, a simple white dress.
Later she holds an intricate cut

glass filled with imported sparkling
wine, sips, smiles. Some men
talk taxes, some dance
with other men's wives.
Each new found
pair wiggles thickened middles hopefully
saying to anyone who stops to watch
"Look at us!" She looks

the perfect audience.
Afterward in the car, he questions her—
he needs to know
what she saw, what she thought.
Each time she says less,
he insists

on more. Then, after they fight,
she ignores his cues, this time escapes
their bed—drawn to
every late night channel—
starts searching for the picture
of that woman inside
the early evening news.

Paranoia

She dreams of an angry animal awaiting her
arrival on an abandoned island
and tries to figure it out
with her paperback Freud.
Sometimes she thinks
the answer lies
in a different source.
Sometimes she's convinced
the accumulated clues add up
to almost nothing.
But mostly she just feels
prey to all the evils

she can imagine,
focuses on every furious
story, remembers each misleading
offering perfect with the promise
of everlasting happiness—
the once upon a time

she was caught
in another person's
spell. Someone gave her token
love which she took
for real,
and it terrifies her
to know
how much she wants to kill.

Amphibians

imaginary gardens with real toads in them

—Marianne Moore

He has her shut her
eyes, imagine a garden,
but all she sees against her lids
is a rough-skinned animal straddling
the border between land and water.
She doesn't want to tell him

in her mind the ontogeny moves
past jellyfish and sponge, down
to cell and disappearance. Once

she heard toads used celestial
bodies for their orientation.
She's come to him
to be her guide, to pull her

forward through his own
perspiration, and he pushes
her to picture
a bird, watch how easily
it takes flight—revel
in the evolution of possibility.
But she is drying

out, his voice too parched
to permeate—she listens to it evaporate
while he still tries to reach her.
His vocal chords open

and close at their given pitch—
small slits in his throat
separate as he says
it's time to go but
we'll meet again next
week; think about envisioning
a sunshower, then a rainbow . . .

Small Green

I do not go away, but the Grounds are ample—
almost travel—.

—Emily Dickinson

She's tried Jungian, Freudian, Transactional
Analyses, even Rolfing, the instructor's knuckles
kneading her skin, fingers pushing up
her nose, fists down
her throat, his dog barking
next to him. She'll tell you the issues

have lodged themselves in her connective tissue
or confide in you about the therapist
who lies in his Naugahyde recliner,
the rips in it camouflaged with masking
tape to keep the stuffing from popping,
and the day he reached deep inside
himself, pulled out his own
caked-on secret, showed it
to her, and how she fled—
because she knew for him there was no cure—
to a braless humanist who played Hindu
music and had her pound
a battered paisley pillow and yell
about her mother and father.
Acquainted with every pamphleteer, she's anchored

herself to a small green chair and watches
neighbors pack their cars for summer travel,
longs to go anywhere, always prepares a bag
twice—once for luck, once to be ready—
and when she doesn't leave, she runs out
to buy the latest self-help book and slowly returns
each folded item to its own familiar shelf.

Agoraphobia

It isn't that she doesn't
want to go to the marketplace, if only
to buy one small
compliment. She can remember each
time she went,
got one, took it
home, put it in
a porcelain cup she kept
beside her bed.
She stopped
going out for fear

of wanting too much to fill
the fragile container,
decorated her house in muted
stripes
and moved onto her bed
a color TV

which she watches
steadily.
She likes the news, especially
the accidents that happen
when people travel too far
from home.
They secure her place.
And when she faces
a scene filled with a good
time, she wanders—
but only in her mind.

The House in Plano

Nature may change; the house rests in its geometric certitude.

—*Franz Schulze* from *Mies van der Rohe, A Critical Biography*

It would be hard to hide in that house
without any cranny to curve into,
unlike here, where each corner provides
a shelter of brick, the view outside almost
a body's throw away. There, the spaces

between the planes and pillars are glass,
the base five feet from the earth,
so it can ignore the river
and its occasional overflow. Nature

fluctuates while that rectangular box holds
firm against slick winds, leaden
snow and the sun on days it burns the rims
of the clouds. Here, in my nook—

a closet of reflection—sometimes only a siren
pulls me out to look onto the street
and even then I draw my shade
as when last week the ambulance shrieked:

lights and noise racing to the widow
in her bungalow across the road,
her small windows draped like closed eyes.
I don't know if she's dead
or alive, can only hope she'll reappear,
that I'll see her, when I glance out, glad

she's been given one more chance
over the forces that flood and push
us back further and finally
down, no wide-flange columns to secure
our floor above the ground.

The Death of a Small Animal

In my child's room
a small animal sickens.
I feed it egg yolk
with an eyedropper every hour.
It eats, then burrows
into bedding of cotton balls.

I remember the first time
death insisted
on something small.
I refused to give it up,
until one day it disappeared.
My parents knew enough
of death to rid
themselves of small reminders.

In my child's room
a small animal lingers
among softness and swallows
yellow liquid.
I stay still
contemplating
its final container.

Creation — The Last Day

In the portal of her sterile
room at the end of a corridor, wearing
the soft cotton gown of hope, she views
babies being carried
to their mothers. Sounds from both sides
of the hall waft through her walls,
even into the bathroom
where they are drowned by the flushing
of blood out the porcelain basin.
Here, she collects her urine
in a jar that by night fills
the air with a salt-water smell
which lingers even after
a nurse carts the liquid away
to test if the fetus is still
alive. She feels she rests

at the bottom of an ocean,
her swollen belly moored
to the hard bed.
In the dark she holds
on to something she'll never be able
to name. After she loses it,

she's given morphine to submerge
the pain and she floats up
to find the cloud
where, as a child, she'd imagined God
watching the world.
The next morning, in her solitary place,
she longs to see what was created
but when she asks, she's told
it's gone—no one could save it.

Since Then

from G. to N.

—Dec. '83

Grace Kelly died last year.
No one told her mother.
They said she wasn't well enough,
wouldn't understand.
Ingrid Bergman died too.
Then for her last performance,
won an Emmy,
which her daughter accepted.

"60 Minutes" questioned Jeffrey MacDonald,
a physician and a Captain,
who wanted so much to fight
in Southeast Asia and instead was sent
to North Carolina where he killed
his wife and daughters.
His mother stays remarkably
proud, denies that it could be.

We have a female astronaut.
She's pretty with the name Sally
Ride—so perfect
it makes some people believe
in individual destiny. Naturally
her family's quite pleased.

Your mother still hopes for some award
for you, while your father boasts
about a daughter you
would not have liked.

I wore a green dress to your funeral.
It felt like the color of guilt. I said
I was dead too.
My parents asked me please
to keep it to myself.

Since then I try
for a few small prizes
wish for some things won—
that anyone who wants to
can idealize.

At the Intersection

There's a fright in the way
she drives, an urgency in how she holds
the wheel; she feels she'll break
apart if she has to yield,
merge, accelerate in order to meet
the ongoing traffic. No one
ever taught her how to ride the highway.
Most familiar with circuitous
routes—inner streets clogged
with stops and starts and caution
signs—when she crawls
she almost invites the honking
cars to crash into her, relives
the tension at the intersection

of the dining and living rooms
after the guests were seated,
being asked to straighten her dress,
pivot—their eyes judging
if she should be blue-ribboned
for pretty. Her heart would gallop
and it'd take hours for her
to slow its beat. Now at every junction
she questions who has the right

of way, how fast she should move—
fears the throbbing underneath if she gets
too excited. It makes her hesitate
at every light, fixate on the glare.
If it's too bright, she backs up,
turns around and goes home.

Dorsey Road

Twelve miles west of here, under
a willow tree, next to a man-made
pond, ducks breeze by our family plot.
I avoid the road
that leads straight there
on my way to shop for groceries
or visit my sister,
steering three blocks east, then north
to a street that skirts
the memories down Dorsey Road—
the fixed signs
of Dunkin' Donuts, Burger King, K Mart,
and the stores that come and go between
the times I find again
I'm part of a slow caravan.
(Repeatedly I tried to take the road
to travel somewhere else,
but always ended up touching
the flat headstones, staring at
the ducks circling in their filtered pool,
vowing to return only if I must.)

When I ride the highway, I race
across its intersection with the road,
hold my breath until the cars moving west
disappear from my rearview mirror.

Given Name

You're speaking of leukemia, melanoma.
"It's similar to these," you say.
"It ends with an 'a'."
You add, "I am going to die."

(Once, I said the same words to you
when a pain would not stop breaking into me
and you replied, "We are all going to die."
Maybe you knew I'd be okay—
now, I feel there's no way
I can say it back to you.)

You say again, "I am going to die,"
this time remembering the name they've given you.
You recite it twice as if you're ten,
in fifth grade—the teacher has called on you
and you have no choice but to stand next
to your desk and answer.
(I reach out to touch your arm,
trying to tell you maybe it's not your turn.)

After Chemotherapy

I bring warm hats,
turquoise and amber,
the brightest I can find
with scarves attached,
so she can wrap her head
and no one will stare.
She tries each on
as if it's the finest gift
I've ever given her,
better than the thirty years
of bracelets and shawls
or even the drawings
rushed home from school
with her name scrawled huge.

Today, her phone call awakens me
and when I speak, her name
comes out too small
and with a question mark.
She interrupts my vague dream
in which she wasn't answering

to say she's going out for a walk,
it's good winter has lasted so long,
everyone's bundled up, no one can see
what's happening to anyone.

Shavings

She cannot reach the arm's length down her body,
so he covers the hassock with a blanket,
lifts her legs, applies the foamy cream,
holds the razor firmly between his index
finger and thumb, his hand quivering.
After he's done—hasn't cut into her—still tense,
he asks "how's it feel, is it good?"—words once
used when they could curl into each other
instead of now when he just gently bundles
her smoothed skin into a towel.

After he cleans the blade, puts it aside,
he grazes her with his eyes and she feels polished
and young. Her mind leaps and bends into
trigonometries of desire. That night she dreams

she's fourteen, holds the shavings
from the bowl she's been carving at school.
The boy next to her is using the plane,
evening the wood for bookends,
shaping them into two huge hearts.
He starts to smile at her and she twirls
toward him, allows him to arch over her,
come as close to her as he can.

Deals with the Universe

I cook lean meat for you to eat,
bring it only as far as your door.
I imagine you under the patchwork
quilt in your room, the sloped ceiling
slowly falling. I am told
that when your mother calls your name,
all you can do is blink.

                At home I unplug
the phone, sheet the TV, tape the face
of the clock, stop keeping track
of any facts, begin making deals
with the Universe: *If I*
sit in my chair, don't move,
you will live through
the afternoon; if I
wash my hair, set it twice,
then start again with fresh
towels, you will get past
the night; if I
only eat foods I hate
it will add another day.

When I find out
they didn't work, I run
to your house to make sure
you aren't there, and discover
your nurse packing her bag, arranging
for her next job. She tells me
"Goodbye" with a full smile, leaves
me alone in your room staring
out your window. Before she disappears
I see her taking wildflowers
from the ground that weeks ago
was too cold to have anything to give.

Flowers

With her thumbs she'd press at the beginning
stems, try to push them back into her chest
as if that could arrest the budding.
Not wanting anyone to see,
so they couldn't point, make fun,
she'd stretch her sweaters
down around her knees,
the yarn slackened and blanketing
her body. She didn't know then that

young men would come with flowers
which felt like the soft skin
of her own grown breasts, their areolas
knowing how to roughen into crinkled leaves,
nipples ruddy. She didn't realize how easily

they all could decay,
that someday they'd be taken from her,
the way she imagined her callers stole
each bloom from its stem, a risk
they took for fantasies of touching her,
their fingers working carefully, anxious
that they'd get in trouble, have to stop—
all blossoms pulled from their hands.

Of Tulips and Trillium

Today they lift a piece of bone
out of him and now in this
immaculate pale room
he can barely exhale.
He's too limp
to smell the blossoms
sent to him or even stare
at his magazine that gleams
with females so much
younger than his youngest daughter—
their magic breasts touched
by anyone who looks.
His face glows
the color of the parts
they don't quite show—
fiery red blooms

of tulips and trillium.
If he'll return home
safe this time, able
to groom this season's flowers
is a question no one can answer.

Each year he'd border our path
with sweet baby pink and crimson—
maybe with the women
in mind that surrounded him—
as he tried to exhibit his love,
quiet his lust.
Now I remember how
we scented the air, making it hard
for him to take a deep breath.

The Picture I Never Gave Her

I'd remember her thick fingers grabbing
at the bows, the flowered
wrappings rumples of agitations
on the floor, and become too frightened

to let her have the last gift.
So I hid it in the sunroom, stared
at its oblong shadow on the rug
like the dark hole dug
for her last June. Crone

in every child book, ravenous
for the little one lost
deep in the thicket—
sometimes I'd wish she'd never
stepped onto the boat, come to this
country. She found the passage too rough
years after she rushed from the dock—
all promises sank against her
huge hopes. Robbers

were what I'd think about
when I'd rehearse handing her my
photograph; how I'd have to steal it back—
enter her apartment, peel it
off the wall some moonless night
while she slept.
Now, she's the one who ransacks

my dreams—caresses
a favorite childhood doll, spins
its head and will
not let me have it.

Stigmata

She'd clutch me to her apron
as the heat from boiling
dinner in the iron kettles
on the stove settled over us
and the windows, closing off
our vision of the street.
She'd pray and wipe
her face and the steam
that coated the panes, so we could hope
to spot everyone safely
returning home. Whenever
anyone was late she'd speak
of some bad lot that could have
befallen them and each night
we'd watch and wait

I'd learn how much there was to dread
when people disappeared
from sight. In our kitchen
a fly would flit from light to light
while we stayed still
as if that might bar every harm
that could occur
before they walked through the door.
They always came home all right—
except the uncle who went

to war, where he was captured,
then freed to return
to our familiar rooms.
Here, he'd sit and stare,
his body bent into the shapes of fear—
stigmata to remind us
of how the world can wound.

Feuerstein

After voices on the radio reported attacks
for over two years, her family
debated, voted, agreed
that the "Feuer" convert to "Fire"
and the "stein" turn into "stone."
In the confusion she sat with relatives
as they signed the papers that allowed
them to appear more American,
her chair part of the arc formed
in front of the cathedral-shaped box that spoke
about a man who wasn't God
who could make people vanish
or fearful enough to give up
their names. Sometimes her grandparents wept
when her mother wrote letters,

read each "how are you we are fine"
out loud, addressed them at first
to Germany, later France and finally
to the International Red Cross.
As they waited in their half circle,

heard more months of news,
her mother used the pen and paper less,
told her the aunts, uncles, cousins
were probably lost, tricked into
boarding trains where there was no time to hide
who they were before they disappeared.

Fourth of July Summer

I'd puff the gummy pink
into a blister, hoping
it'd grow bigger
than the last—cover
my face before it exploded
over my hair and chin.
Then, I'd imagine the judge's shout
Winner and there I'd be on stage
to receive the prize,
while my cousins would watch
and wish they'd practiced more.
Only the competition

never happened, because the paperboy,
a man the adults whispered about,
called retarded, demolished
his arm with a homemade bomb
and all fireworks, celebrations
were banned. We never saw him again

ride his overgrown tricycle, its huge
baskets hinged to the back fenders.
He'd deliver the news—words
we'd hear over and over:
MacArthur, Okinawa, Japan—
hand our mothers their evening
reading while they talked about lost
relatives in Europe. We searched
for the comics, poked
our fingers into the holes
of the pastel-painted steel chairs
they sat in, wrestled
for their attention and counted

the days until our fathers could escape
the city, race to the country
and to us—more Jews gathered
on the bluff, running down
the wooden steps to the edge
of Lake Michigan, dipping
our toes into the cold
water, hollering to one another.
It was the summer the air vibrated

with cancellations: the marching
bands with majorettes tossing
their batons higher
and higher, the bubble-blowing
contest, the carnival of colored fire.

Sophie

Born December 25th, or so she chooses
to say, in a Russian town whose name
she slurs so no one knows exactly
where, she left her family
at fourteen to marry a distant cousin.
On the boat, she tells clearly,
the Captain gave her
extra food for the pleasure he took
in her smile.
But her mother-in-law-to-be dismissed her
appeals and would not allow
the marriage to the son who would become
"the very rich American."
Exiled in her new country, Sophie found
Harry in the back room
of a kosher butcher shop, playing cards
and losing.

Today, she's eighty-three,
with daughters who phone her
twice a day and have never moved
more than twenty miles away.
Three generations
bring gifts, wish
her Happy Birthday. She thanks them,
says how much
they're loved, forgives each
neglect. She reminds them
of the sacrifice.

They continue the unsettled
disappointments in her alien
land, for which she left
her parents, brothers, sisters:
the family she wanted back and found,
long after she sailed away,
on a list labeled "Lost."

Lana Turner in the
Butcher Shop

He'd sit between the slabs of meat
in the basement freezer of the butcher shop—
his hiding place a wooden chair
with a pack of cigarettes
taped underneath the seat.
There he'd smoke his heart out,
blow the pain into the cold dark
air, watch the puffs cloud
the hanging carcasses.

Upstairs his wife would take care
of the customers. "Dressed to kill,"
some would whisper
as they'd watch her in the finest
knit sweater and skirt.
She'd weigh the ground beef,
wrap it, mark it, hand it over
with her Lana Turner smile—move
across the sawdust floor
as if dancing on stardust.
Only at home would she shout—
then race out to buy another
purse or dress or pair of shoes.

Thirty years before, she'd worn
the best lace ruffles in Russia
and listened to her family fuss
about how she was the prettiest.
At the same time in Germany, he'd proudly
carried his anatomy
books with strong and graceful hands.
Then they left on different boats,
only to end up together
in the same unimagined land.

HOllycourt 5-7434

The phone is still connected
but if I call she won't answer.
Soon the movers will haul the furniture
away like the paramedics carted her
through the hall, down the torn green
carpeted stairs and finally
into the fresh air where they kept pressing
her chest, her huge breasts tossed
to her sides—she used to fold them
into her brassiere and years before,
when corsets were the fashion, lace them
tight up against her heart
so she wouldn't attract the wrong attentions.
In the moment on the sidewalk people stared

but stayed put—in this neighborhood
all deaths are considered
contagious. From their separate stoops
a few old men strained to hear
the women guess who it was and how
it happened. Now it's quiet

on the second floor where for months
children and grandchildren called
the doctor and the pharmacist—
interpreted an old woman's despair—
and a visiting nurse with steady hands
came twice a week to wash her
in a tub of shallow water.
She was the baby in the family

some seventy years ago, so healthy and round
at fourteen when her parents let her go
for the safety and the promise
of the "new country." They packed her gifts
that overflowed with memories,
and when I'm asked would I like to have some

Prussian china plates, all that's left
is to say yes
because she carried them with her
from a place that can no longer be reached.

Anna of Devon Avenue

From a patrolled town in the Ukraine
to Baltimore on a boat, then a train to Chicago,
she came to the road that runs
from Boychik's Restaurant to Weinstein's Mortuary.
Here she moved easily in and out
of every store, stopped anyone she recognized
for some talk, wheeled
daughters, granddaughters, great-grandsons
up and down the sidewalk. For seventy years,
day after day, she traveled this route, watched
Manzelman's Market, Mr. Savitsky's Butcher Shop,
Meyer the tailor disappear,
made up her own way
of saying Taj Sari Palace, Gujarat's Grocers,
Psistaria Grecian Imports and once at
Kwong Seng Lo even ate an eggroll,
probably laced with pork.
The last time she strolled
on her street, she hugged

her shopping bag too tight, broke
a rib that forced her inside.
The morning she died she awoke early, pushed
a chair as close as she could to the window
that overlooked the avenue, sat down and stared,
saw her dead husband coming home, tired
from unloading trucks at Sears,
cousins she hadn't thought about in years,
their bosoms covered by flowered aprons,
breathing hard, rushing up
the stairs with stories to tell. She exhaled
their names: Simon, Sadye, Rosie, Belle,
and felt her own slip out
of herself, drift and settle
in place—five blocks east, three blocks west.

Psalm

The rabbi davens over a grave
audience. Some already dead listen
beneath the ground—my grandfather,
not frightened as he was in his hospital
gown, wears the brown suit
he wore to Passover eleven days before
he died. When I cried too much
I heard him breathe

"*Shah. Shah.*" My cousin deciphers
his expressions—for eight years
she's been soothed by his good company.
They never spoke in that other life.
Here, she talks to him about time
she's lost—tells me too
in so many dreams. I thought
I'd have to go, be with her to calm

me down. Today we bury
an aunt, place her next
to the husband who has not noticed her yet.
My grandfather greets her with an *"Oy gevalt"*
and then a kiss—
even after eighteen years
he's not quite used to death.
Finally, her husband turns
toward her and asks
about their family, but she doesn't answer—

her incisions still too fresh. The ground
beneath the canopy holds us awhile
and the rabbi hymns the psalm.
My grandfather whispers
"Gey, zie strong
if you can—if not, then here
is where I am."

The Astonishment of Being Alive

*Yesterday your letter arrived and this poem
is my reply.*

The rumormonger's twisted voice carried
me the message that you'd died
and when I yelled *No.*
No. Not Possible. and couldn't
quit, she finally cowered and left
against the din. Ten years

you traveled to me while I slept,
lay against my narrow blanket,
kept whispering *stay, I am*
alive. I came so close to sealing
my eyes, the garage door.
I'd feel the motor running
wild—an arrhythmia, then burst
of the heart. I knew a woman
who did it before dinner.
She passed the cooking food,
the set table, stepped into
her favorite blue dress
and slipped away quickly with
the carburetor pumping death.
For months I wouldn't wear that color
as if that could force me
to become her. My cousin did

a slow tango with cancer.
Then, he took her as his
trophy—a small copper box
cupped in his palm. I too felt
the crush. But you ran
after the angel, able to
crumple his wings, heal
over the forever days

to now and this letter
I read again and again.
It lies so gentle in my hand,
the thin paper, the thick script.
I see *love,* my name and you
the boy, the man and our odd story
which is itself many
stories. Second, Third, Fourth
Chances. Together we'll have
eighteen lives. You've come back
at least the once you've described.
I've come back myself, twice.
Some mud still sticks to my fingertips,
but today I am astonished
by the world, how huge
the word happiness.

for S.